DESERT MISSION

First Published by ICON Communications Ltd., 1990

Designed by Ted and Ursula O'Brien, Oben Design.
Phototypeset by Oben in 11pt. *CG Palacio* on Compugraphic® MCS8200.
Colour Reproduction by Masterphoto Engraving Ltd.
Printed in Ireland.

ISBN 0 9515773 0 1

DESERT MISSION
Twenty-five years in Peru

Text by
Tim Cramer

Photography by
Richard Mills

Published by
ICON Communications

Most Rev. Dr. Cornelius Lucey, D.D.
Former Bishop of Cork & Ross and founder of the Diocesan
Mission in Peru.

Ven. Archdeacon Thomas Duggan
Archdeacon Duggan volunteered for the Peru Mission at an
advanced age and died in Lima six weeks after his arrival there.

Introduction

HE WAS over eighty years old. Or so he told me. He wasn't sure, however. In fact, he looked much older. Two of his grandchildren had come running to the house that morning: "Come quickly, Padre!" they said, "our *abuelo* is dying!" "Where do you live?" I asked. "Come on, we'll show you", they answered willingly.

I put them into the back of our battered Volkswagen Beetle, gathered the Oil of the Sick, a Prayerbook and Stole, brought the Blessed Sacrament from the church, and set off. The streets of the shanty-town, laid out in parallel lines, criss-crossed at the end of every block. The surface was sandy, some streets hardened by constant traffic while others, less travelled, were treacherous to motor vehicles. Unexpected patches of deep soft sand could lead to the car sinking to the axles. Such streets were to be avoided. But when one is in a hurry, caution is often thrown to the wind. The consequences are frustrating!

"What is the name of your street?" I asked my guides, who, not over-concerned now about the eternal salvation of their grandfather, were enjoying a rare drive in a car. "Atahualpa", they chorussed. Atahualpa was a famous Inca leader, treacherously murdered by the soldiers of the Spanish conqueror Pizarro almost 450 years before. Many streets in Peru bear the names of heroes of various eras from the past. It is not uncommon, however, to come across streets, particularly in the shanty-towns, carrying names like 'The 9th of September', 'The 14th of May' and so on. The dates immortalised in this way sometimes refer to notable dates in the history of the country. More often, they refer to the date on which 'invasions' took place. The 'invasions' in question are the arrival of a large group of people, generally from the same *pueblo* in the mountains, to stake their claim to a patch of desert on the fringe of the shanty-town. The date of such an invasion when, overnight, they mark out lots, build straw huts and raise the national flag, is a significant date for the people involved.

Having successfully negotiated various deep patches of sand, my guides and I arrived at one of these straw huts. The family had migrated from the mountains a few months before, bringing with them all their worldly possessions. The straw hut had three small rooms, one of which was a 'bedroom'. It was there I found the *abuelo*, lying on a piece of straw-matting on the sandy floor and covered with a blanket.

He was old alright, but then it is hard to judge a Peruvian's age. He might have been about 50; he looked 100; he said he was 80. Two dark eyes peered at me from a wrinkled and emaciated face. He spoke to me of his *pueblo*, his native place, high in the Andes. Most of his life had been spent there, struggling to support his family. When I asked him how he made his living, his answer surprised me: ''I worked the mines by day, and I worked the land by night'', he said. ''When did you sleep'', I asked. ''I didn't'', he answered; ''I never slept for almost 40 years''.

A real Rip Van Winkle in reverse, I thought to myself. Either the man was hallucinating or my imagination was being stretched to the limit! ''How did you manage to stay awake?'' I asked, with a hint of incredulity in my voice. ''The *coca* leaf'', he said, ''I used to chew the *coca* leaf. It takes away the hunger and the need for sleep''. I had heard that the *coca* plant, which grows wild on the mountains, could have such effects, yet it was hard to believe his story, whatever his age. One thing was certain — his life hadn't been easy. Now that it was coming to an end, he wanted to see the priest, to confess his sins and to receive the Sacraments of the Church.

His native village was remote, he told me, and there had been no priest there for many years, apart from the annual *fiesta* when a priest was 'hired' from the coast for a week. He had scarcely been in a church since the day his youngest child had been christened — and that was 45 years ago. But his basic belief was Catholic, and now, as he approached death, he was anxious to put things right. He still remembered the ordinary prayers, taught to him by his parents all those years ago, and obviously repeated through the long days and nights as he worked to raise his family.

A broad smile creased his wrinkled face when he received the Sacred Host. ''I'm happy now'', he said, ''God has been very good to me''. I thought of Simeon and I was humbled.

As I drove slowly away from the straw hut, my mind was full of thoughts of Providence. The ways of the Lord are strange and wonderful, I mused; that my life and the old man's should touch at this point; that across thousands of miles and so many years, he and I should meet . . .

Harsh reality awakened me from my reverie. As I turned the corner, the car sank into the fine sand! An hour later, with the help and advice of a group of local youths, and soaked in a mixture of perspiration and dust, I was on my way again. Cautiously I drove back to the house, hoping there would be enough water to allow me to take a shower.

Getting out of the car, I heard the shout ''Padre! Padre!'' came the young voices. It was the two grandchildren again. ''What's up?'' I asked. ''Our *abuelo* died about ten minutes ago'', was their reply.

Liam O'Driscoll.

Preface

IN PERU there is plenty of time. *Mañana* never comes, and yet, waiting for tomorrow, hoping for better things is part of the culture. As I look back over 25 years of involvement in the shanty-towns of Trujillo, I begin to wonder: where has the time gone? And yet, it only seems like yesterday since it all began! It is impossible to quantify what has been achieved in those years; what has happened is that all of us who have worked there have been immeasurably enriched by the experience. Peru has become much more than a faraway place; it is towns, streets, houses, people, friends.

I thank God for the many blessings he has given us and the people of the shanty-towns since 1965. Looking now at the situation there, it is very evident that the needs are just as great, if not greater, than when we began. A much bigger population as well as a struggling economy are responsible for that. Each time I visit our parishes there, the people continue to insist that we remain and work among them. And we intend to remain until such time as we can be sure that Peruvian priests and sisters are ready to take our place.

As I reflect on the last 25 years, I am very aware that a whole new generation has grown up here at home who need to be informed about Peru, its people and our involvement there. Since our efforts in Peru over the years could not have continued without the extraordinary generosity of the people of Cork and Ross, we have an obligation to keep them informed about the work they support. This book is part of that effort — to help you, the reader, to reach an understanding of Peru and its character.

I congratulate all concerned with this fine publication, and I feel sure that it will make its own contribution to the ongoing success of our missionary endeavour.

Michael Murphy, Bishop of Cork & Ross.
March, 1990.

Acknowledgements

ANY BOOK is necessarily the product of many hands and many minds. Every author owes a debt of gratitude to people without whom his own efforts would be that much poorer, that much less readable. I am no exception. First, I must thank Most Rev. Dr. Murphy, Bishop of Cork and Ross, for inviting me to Peru to see the work of the mission at first hand and for the many kindnesses and the great hospitality I received from him, from the clergy and from the Sisters during that visit.

Fr. Liam O'Driscoll, head of the Diocesan Communications Office, has been a veritable tower of strength, in providing sources of information, in reading proofs and suggesting necessary amendments and not least, in his encouragement and unfailing courtesy and good humour. My thanks also to the Secretarial staff of the Diocesan Communications Office.

Not all of these writings are my own; some are culled from the work of others over the years, from the time of the late Dr. Lucey to the present day and in this respect, I must thank the many priests who so gladly made their own scholarship available to me; allowed me to see and use their writings and took time to speak to me about Peru and the work of the mission. I owe them all a deep debt of gratitude.

A word about people. The work of the Peru mission is necessarily a team effort and its success reflects on everyone who has served there. It has, for historical reasons, been necessary to mention some, especially perhaps the pioneers, while omitting many who followed, yet who have interesting tales to tell and whose own contribution has been no less. They would, I know, eschew publicity. Nevertheless, I must thank them for their support and understanding of the problem of trying to get the proverbial quart into the pint pot.

Finally, I must thank Ted and Ursula O'Brien and Paul Bennett of Oben Design for their expertise and their invaluable work in the area of typesetting, layout and design; Matt O'Connor and Joe McHugh for their continuing interest and assistance; and colleague Richard Mills for his remarkable photographs, the 'selection from strength' of which caused us all much soul-searching!

A list of our sponsors appears at the end of the book.

Tim Cramer
March 1990.

ECUADOR

COLUMBIA

BRAZIL

● Trujillo

PERU

■ Lima

● Cuzco

BOLIVIA

South
America

PERU

■ Coastal Desert

■ Sierra, or mountains

□ Amazonian jungle

A typical valley in the mountains, where the mighty Andes tower majestically above a landscape that has not changed for centuries. In such places, the huge condor spreads his black wings, tipped with white and spanning up to ten feet.

Facing page: An old doorway frames a mountain village.

Where the Condor Soars

PERU? Oh yes, that's somewhere in South America. Or, Peru? Isn't that the long skinny bit that runs down the Pacific coast? (No, it is not!) So location, it seems, is important. Before beginning to consider any country, especially one so remote, it is as well to define exactly where it is, and possibly the best way to do this is by classic textbook definition.

Peru is situated on the western (Pacific) coast of South America between 4 and 18 degrees south of the Equator. It is bounded on the north by Ecuador, on the north-east by Colombia, on the east by Brazil; the south-east by Bolivia and on the south by Chile (the long skinny bit). Better still, look at the accompanying map, which puts Peru in its proper perspective, better than any words can.

Physically, like Caesar's Gaul of old, it is divided into three parts: desert coastline, mountain or sierra (the Andes, which run like a huge spine down through the country) and steamy jungle, which is on the eastern side of the Andes and from which springs the mighty Amazon, in a whole series of root-like tributaries.

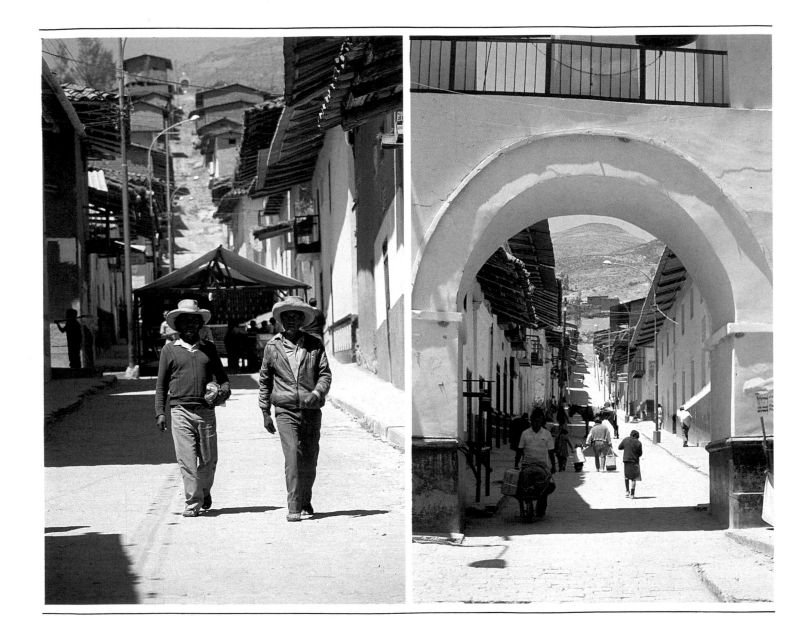

Deeply overhanging eaves, steep narrow streets and ornate wooden balconies characterise mountain villages like Otusco, fifty miles from Trujillo. Sierra dwellers are colourful, hardy people, but life is difficult, with few facilities.

THREE

These divisions, of course, mean three distinct types of climate, with varying degrees of discomfort as one moves from one to the other. The coastline for instance, tends to be very dry and unproductive. In fact, much of this strip is mere desert, even though along here are situated the capital, Lima and important cities like Trujillo, together with the large port of Callao, outside Lima and the Dante-like inferno of industrial Chimbote.

This coastline tends to be hot, especially in the summer, which is from December to March, but it is a dry heat with little humidity and the area is cooled somewhat by the Pacific breezes and by the cold current from the Antarctic, named after its discoverer, Humboldt.

Rainfall here is minimal. It has rained 'properly' only twice this century, in 1925 and in 1981. Consequently there is not a great deal of cultivation along this narrow strip of land, except where it adjoins the foothills of the Andes, and where the occasional river makes its way to the sea. These river valleys, usually growing sugar cane and vegetables, illustrate the fertility of the Peruvian desert, which, if irrigated, can produce three crops annually.

The sierra, by and large, tends to be more comfortable for the visitor, with its clean, dry air, but this in turn can lead to altitude sickness in very high places like Cuzco and Machu Picchu, the ancient city of the Incas, where the air is so thin that acclimatisation is essential and where oxygen masks are regularly doled out to tourists on the slow train to the Inca ruins.

It is from the high sierra that many of the people in this story come, from tiny holdings in mountain fastnesses and from little villages that seem to belong to another age. It is from here also that the now notorious *Sendero Luminoso* or Shining Path Maoist guerillas operate, waging their vicious war on an innocent population, of which more in succeeding chapters.

Inland, on the eastern side of the sierra, is the dense tropical jungle, where the climate is such that it can only be described as inhumanly steamy; where the visitor is constantly quite literally pouring with perspiration and where all the dangers of tropical disease are most apparant, together of course with the exotic flora and fauna of the jungle.

The whole country is divided into Departments or Regions, of which there are 25 in all, with an estimated population of some 20 million — estimated because exact figures are extremely difficult to realise because of migration or 'invasion' of the cities by those seeking a better way of life.

The Department of La Libertad (pop. 1.5 million) of which Trujillo is the capital, is that which concerns us mainly, because it is here that the Cork and Ross Diocesan Mission is situated, some 350 miles north of Lima. Here, in the desert, are the *pueblos jovenes* (new

Peruvian backs are strong, carrying everything from children to bags of produce.
In Southern Peru, the mountain railway too is a carrier, always attracting crowds.

towns) or shanty towns of the very poor and here the Cork priests and nuns are to be found. This is their story, as well as that of Peru itself, a land of turbulent past and uncertain future, where life seems to move in rhythm with the slow beat of the wings of the giant condor, the bird which has become so much a symbol of Peru.

Trujillo is very much a Spanish-colonial city, with its elegant Plaza de Armas in the centre, its lovely, white-faced cathedral and its municipal buildings. Delicate wrought-iron work characterises the windows, and old timber balconies abound. Beyond this, the city is divided sharply into the areas of 'have' and 'have not'. The buildings in one are of *material noblé* or solid brick and stone; in the other are the *adobé* huts and straw shanties of the poor and the very poor.

These are the new towns of the desert, the ever-growing areas of population of a people desperate for even the most basic facilities — and a little hope.

Modern lamp-posts bring a strange incongruity to an old village street.

Facing page: Strong sunlight dapples an Andean valley but the muddy waters of the near dried-up river bed are scarcely inviting. The road is typical of its kind, unpaved and unfenced.

Above: A familiar form of transport in the sierra.

Top left: A typical small home in the mountains, built from adobe or mud bricks. It may look pictursesque, but conditions here are very basic and a meagre living has to be scratched from stony soil.

Bottom left: A burro (mule) rests in a doorway while waiting to be unloaded. In a land where mañana rules, he may well need his Peruvian patience.

Facing page: Part of the great Pan-American highway, the only land link between the capital Lima and Trujillo. It is allegedly possible to drive the Pan-American almost from Cape Horn to Alaska. Long it may be; wide it rarely is, as the picture shows. Some stretches are also bandit-infested.

Above and left: Among the better legacies left by the Spanish colonists are some fine buildings with highly ornate wrought-iron windows. Many of them are well preserved, like these in the centre of Trujillo.

Facing page: Spanish-colonial style architecture shows its finest face in the Cathedral, situated in the Plaza de Armas (main square) in Trujillo.

ELEVEN

An early picture of one of the 'pueblos jovenes' or new towns, springing up in the desert outside Trujillo about the time of the foundation of the mission.

Much the same scene pictured 24 years later, in 1989. The community has settled, some basic services have been provided and a few of the homes have even acquired upper storeys.

Above: Arrival point of one of the newer 'invasions' in the desert outside Trujillo. Here the tiny homes are built of 'esteras' (straw matting).

Facing page: Reeds are used in constructing the boats used by the fishermen of Huanchaco, on the Pacific coast.

Above: The fabled Inca 'lost city' of Machu Picchu perched high in the Andes near Cuzco in Southern Peru. Now only the ghosts of a proud, civilised people, massacred by the Spanish Conquistadores, occupy what was once their citadel.

Facing page: Most Peruvians love to be photographed — even if the smile is a little toothless!

Land of Culture, Coups and Chaos

IT IS common, when considering Peruvian history, to focus on the colourful Incas and the Spanish conquest. Long before the emergence of the Inca domination however, there existed in Peru other, older civilisations, traces of which still remain. The Mochicas, for instance, worked in pottery and metal; artefacts depicting their way of life have been found in relative abundance.

Near Trujillo is one of the vast *adobé* (mud brick) palaces of the Chimu, who existed about seven centuries ago and who succeeded the Mochicas. Its walls are still emblazoned with the twin symbols of fish and pelican, the latter being their emblem — and perhaps hope — of plenty. Covering hundreds of acres, its intricate system of building reflects a highly organised, hierarchical structure. It is claimed to be the largest mud city in the world.

Again, the Nazca people marked the desert with strange line patterns which are visible only from the air and which are now the subject of much scholarship and speculation. Yet another race, the Paracas, seem to have been sophisticated enough to practice brain

Facing page: General view of a small portion of the huge complex at Chan-Chan, where restoration work is still continuing.

Above and right: Intricate symbolic carvings on the walls of the mud palaces at Chan-Chan, outside Trujillo. The main symbols are those of fish and pelican.

surgery, evidence of which has been found in their burial sites.

These were some of the cultures, each emerging over the ages, flourishing and subsiding or being vanquished in Peru's bloody history. Inevitably, because of fabled Machu Picchu, of legendary vast wealth of precious metals and of the savage subjugation by the Conquistadores, the Incas continue to this day to hold centre stage in the long Peruvian drama.

When the loutish and brutal swineherd Francisco Pizarro arrived with 180 men at Tumbes in northern Peru in 1532, the Inca kingdom had long been something of a South American superpower, its empire stretching from Colombia to Chile. The rule of the sun-worshipping Incas was both feudal and authoritarian, but it did provide food and employment for all.

Looking at it contemporaneously, however, by 1532 it is an empire wracked by plague and civil war between two royal brothers, Huascar and Atahualpa, eventual victor in the struggle. Pizzaro is able to take full advantage of the chaos and so, amazingly, conquers a whole empire with his handful of men. Tricked, kidnapped and ransomed for a room-full of gold, Atahualpa is shamefully murdered anyway and hundreds of unarmed Incas are massacred. It is the end of native rule in Peru.

Swiftly, driven by extreme greed, the Spanish colonists take over, sending the natives down the mines to extract gold, silver and mercury. Much of the irrigated land on the coast was lost when expert native irrigators were sent down the mines. They died young and their expertise died with them. The effects of this are still evident.

In this terrible forced labour, two million people have died by 1600, victims of Spanish gold-lust and European disease. In addition, the colonists have taken over all the Indian lands and build huge ranches or *haciendas*. Lima, the capital, has become the seat of the Inquisition.

There is some sporadic resistance. In 1780, Tupac Amaru II, an Inca descendant, leads a rebellion which ends in disaster, with thousands killed, including Amaru and his family. Many more are deported.

When independence finally does come, after years of savage repression, it is largely outsiders who achieve it — Argentinians, Venezuelans and Colombians — and it is an Argentinian, Jose de San Martin, who raises the flag of freedom over Lima in 1821 and formally declares independence. But turbulent Peru's troubles are only beginning.

The exploitation and sale of so unlikely a commodity as *guano* — bird manure — along with the country's other rich natural resources, by a new breed of capitalists, transforms the economy but most of the money finds its way into the Bank of England and few Peruvians benefit. In 1879, Peru declares itself bankrupt.

*The Pyramid of the Sun, one of two pyramids built by the
Mochicas, an early Peruvian civilisation.*

Peruvians work at whatever occupation they can find, from cobbling to car-washing to selling fruit. Note the inventive use of plastic crates for stall construction.

Yet more capitalists emerge to rebuild the economy and by 1883 a powerful oligarchy of some 50 families attract American support and take over the rich mining and oil interests. But by 1919 low wages and appalling conditions see the emergence of trade unions, of strikes and violence and of two main political parties, APRA (American Revolutionary Alliance Party), and the Communist Party. There follows a whole succession of power struggles, coups, mass murders and mayhem.

In 1930 army officer Luis Sanchez Cerro seizes power and dismantles the unions. Protesting miners are ruthlessly killed and in one notorious incident in 1932, one thousand APRA activists are shot by the army.

Fascist Oscar Benavides takes power, only to be succeeded by another dictator, General Manuel Odria in 1948. Whatever his shortcomings, Peru industrialises rapidly and by the end of his rule has attracted much foreign capital. The year 1962 sees another leader, Fernando Belaunde of the conservative Popular Action Party. He soon has to face the emergence of a guerilla organisation of APRA dissidents, the MIR. Using napalm, supplied by the United States, he puts them down ruthlessly, together with many innocent peasants. Not surprisingly, his government soon sinks into division, corruption and unpopularity.

The political swings and roundabouts continue. In 1968 General Juan Velasco takes over and enforces land

A young lad gives a demonstration of the haunting 'pipes of pan' which are an integral part of Peru's musical culture.

reform — the first real break with Spanish colonial economic policy. But he falls ill in 1975 and the economic situation quickly deteriorates. Riots in Lima lead to 200 deaths. Enter, by way of a bloodless coup, General Francisco Morales Bermudes and the government swings to the right.

There follow yet more years of unrest, strikes and crippling price rises. By 1980, Belaunde's PAP is re-elected, but by now too the Maoist 'Shining Path' guerillas have emerged, taking over the town of Ayacucho. In the ensuing imposition of a state of emergency, many atrocities are committed by the armed forces.

On to the troubled scene in 1985 strides APRA leader, the charismatic, Kennedy-like Alan Garcia, full of hope and promise. The hope is short-lived, the promise vain. By 1989, the Peruvian economy is in tatters. The foreign debt repayments have been reneged, the banks and insurance companies nationalised. Inflation is running at a rate unimagined even by hardened economists and the life of the ordinary people has become incredibly difficult, even by their standards. The country seems ripe for revolution — except that nobody, it seems, wants to undertake a coup and all the attendant, monumental problems of government.

Two students from Trujillo dance the traditional Marinera, a beautiful Peruvian love-dance.

Peruvians are a gregarious people, always ready to gather
in groups for a chat and ever-colourful in their traditional clothing.

A Warm and Worthy People

IT IS dawn. The first rays of a blood-orange sun reach over the Andes and bounce off the Cathedral in Trujillo, turning its white facade into a dome of shimmering gold. In the little reed hut in the *barriada* there is no sunlight yet. Maria stirs, wakes and sighs, conscious of the long, hard day ahead. She is lonely. Her husband has 'gone away', a euphemism for desertion. Today will be like any other, a battle for survival. Then she looks over at the little tousled head above the pile of old clothes and smiles. She has one treasure at least. Suddenly, a ray of sunlight penetrates the woven grass . . .

Maria is like thousands of other Peruvians. No matter how appalling the conditions in which many of them are compelled to live, there remains a spark of humour, the well of hospitality, the determination to overcome adversity and to carry on, regardless of the fact that they may not know where the next meal is coming from.

They are a hardy and optimistic race, these people whose heritage and tradition go back to the very dawn of time. They are, today, part Spanish, part Indian, *mestizo*, or mixed race, and while some look very

Spanish and others very Indian, it would be very difficult to assess just what a true Peruvian actually is.

You would insult a Peruvian by calling him *cholo*, a derogatory term for one of mixed race, and then he will reply by calling you *gringo* or foreigner. Mostly, this latter term is affectionate and used fairly frequently in that manner, but ever and anon, the frustration about what the *gringos* have done to their country breaks out. Then it is said with some venom, especially when it refers to Americans, for whom the worst antagonism seems to be reserved at present.

But by and large, the Peruvian will welcome you into his home and his family, even though his home may be very small and poor and his family very large and hungry. He and his wife will try to share what little they have and that tends to create a dilemma. To accept is to deprive them, and anyway the food may not exactly suit Western tummies; to refuse may be to insult them, even though they are very slow to anger.

Peruvian children especially, are very lovable. Walk into a schoolyard and you will be surrounded by tots who will all want to be picked up and hugged, who will look in black-eyed wonder at these strange white people who have come to visit them, but who will all too quickly overcome their shyness and cluster around, shouting greetings. And just when you think you have embraced everybody, you will see a little face at the

The cheerful smile of this Indian lady (opposite) reflects optimism in the face of adversity. The gentleman above seems to be taking life a little more seriously.

Studies in expression (above and facing page) as young Peruvians are captured by the camera.

back of the crowd and a sad pair of eyes which seem to say: "What's wrong with me, why did I get no hug?"

They are, of course, dreadful rogues, these Peruvians. In the majority of places, you may walk safely among them, even in the *barriadas*, without fear for personal safety. But they are also extremely poor, and you will be foolish indeed if you carry your money in any reasonably accessible place, such as a back pocket or an open handbag. Desperate situations, it must be remembered, create desperate needs.

Not all Peruvians, of course, are poor. In the cities, such as Lima and Trujillo, there are houses comparable in luxury to those to be found anywhere and here there are people who are wealthy and urbane, as welcoming as the others, provided you are known to them and of their 'class'. They will throw their homes open to you, but most would shudder even to think of going near a *barriada*.

"El Porvenir" said one young lady in horror, "I would never go there''. When it was gently pointed out that real people lived there, the answer was the same. Beyond the confines of the luxury living on the right side of the tracks, the world ceased, abruptly. Yet, there are one or two who actively assist the Cork missionaries, with professional advice and with the resolution of problems; who seem to have a genuine interest in improving the lot of the less fortunate. They are rare,

Facing page: The elderly are usually resigned to their lot, especially the women, who do most of the work.

Above: Straw hats ward off the worst of the hot sun.

but their commitment is typically whole-hearted.

Peruvian society, it seems, is sharply divided into two classes, the 'haves' and the 'have nots', but the latter are very much in the majority. These are the people who concern us most here, the migrants from the mountains, the very poor, the totally underprivileged. Almost 70 per cent of the population is now urban, a complete reverse of the situation 40 years ago, and the cities are utterly unable to cope with this influx. Most have a life expectancy of about 58, as against 70 in the west. Child mortality rate is 172 per thousand, as against 9 in Ireland. Some 125,000 have emigrated in the last three years. They are the fortunate ones perhaps.

Most are Spanish-speaking, though other minority languages such as Quechua and Aymara are still spoken in remote areas and among those who come from them in ever increasing numbers. Most would claim to be Catholic — a result of the Spanish conquest, and those who are actually practising are very devout. Many simply do not have the opportunity. Again, other sects from the 'Bible belt' of the United States are arriving in ever increasing numbers and offering all sorts of inducements for conversion — without any of the necessary social back-up such as schools and hospitals. Their churches and temples — few in number — are mostly ill-attended.

But all poor Peruvians are imbued with one hope: to break out of the endless grind of poverty and provide education and a better life for their children. These are the people, rascally, warm-hearted, lovable, to whom the Cork and Ross mission is reaching out, bringing the message of eternal love and as much of the material benefits of modern society as can be managed.

Left and facing page: "You youngsters may be able to laugh now, but life gets harder as you grow older"; two pictures showing contrast and character.

Above: A family strolls home to their straw hut in one of the new shanty towns under the mountain outside Trujillo.

Facing page: Two ladies survey the scene from the 'doorway' of a tiny home.

Work, Scrounge, Steal or Starve

LIVING conditions in the *pueblos jovenes* (new towns), and indeed in all areas of Peru except those in which the few privileged live, must surely be similar to those in the depressed areas of this country a hundred years ago. People live in the most primitive accommodation, without any water, sanitation, proper cooking facilities or indeed any vestige of modern comfort. Disease, including tuberculosis and typhoid, is an ever-present threat and death is never very far away, especially for the very young and the feeble elderly.

The interiors of all the shanty-town huts are very similar: a mud or sand floor, depending on the locality, makeshift furniture, very often built from old boxes with a few old clothes thrown on the beds, very little light and even less room to move about. Generally, they tend to be one-roomed, though a sleeping area may be curtained off. Even in the larger adobe huts of those who are clawing their way to some minimal sort of living, the conditions remain depressing.

From these tiny, uncomfortable abodes that are called home, the average Peruvian makes his or her dreary way to another day's work each morning — though 'work' in this context means simply whatever they can

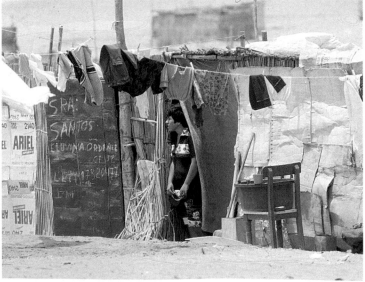

find to do. Few have regular employment in the sense in which it is known in the West. Much of the work is necessarily done by the women, firstly because of the dire unemployment situation; secondly because many of the men have gone off with other 'wives' anyway. Those who are left in charge of young families have to scrape what living they can, and this includes older children who often make a considerable contribution to the meagre income of the household.

You will find them in the streets of Trujillo, washing cars, shining shoes, hawking little trays of matches, or if they can afford to buy the raw materials, cooked or uncooked foods. Curiously, in such a situation, there are fewer beggars than might be expected; the majority prefer to earn and anyway, there are very few people from whom to beg, because almost nobody has the proverbial 'spare penny'.

So it is not uncommon, on a stroll through the streets, to find a man carrying a live turkey, another a piglet, or a woman with an armful of cabbages, on the way to a market where no sale may be made, just as sometimes happened at the fairs in Ireland years ago. Others, a little more prosperous, come to the open-air markets with their produce piled on three-wheeled bicycle carts, which are such a feature of the local scene. If they have a good day, the same tricycles are used for transport home in the evening.

Facing page: Washing is usually a communal occasion and fortunately, everything dries quickly in the hot sun.

Life in the barriadas is not easy, but this lady (above) at least has a proper cooking stove.

On the road to the mountain village of Otusco, where there is an obligatory stop at a police checkpoint about halfway up the mountain, women will crowd around the vehicle, offering little bunches of tattered, tired herbs, flowers and perhaps some food, which few would even give a second glance, let alone be tempted to buy. Such is the desperation of daily living in this beautiful but impoverished land.

Outside Trujillo, it is a harrowing sight to see people, young and old alike, scavenging the local dump, sharing the few spoils with a herd of pigs bent on the same purpose. Even the apparently most useless bits and pieces are garnered because here, everything is put to some sort of use eventually; everything is precious to somebody.

The majority of those who have left the mountains, attracted by the bright lights of the coast and the all too often vain prospect of better times, have left the sierra for good. They may romance, as do we all, about the 'good old days' in the mountains, but if the whole family has left, they never go back. Others, who still have relatives in the hills, may have kept their little patch of land, which is still tilled and from which the produce they sell in Trujillo comes. They are the more fortunate ones; at least they have some tiny source of income.

The other traders have to buy wherever they can and

Above and facing page: Little stalls of produce are everywhere
but, as always, cash is tight and careful choice is essential —
except, of course, for some . . . .

Facing page: The poor of Trujillo indulge in any sort of occupation likely to provide a living.

Above: Hopeful vendors try to tempt a truck driver on a mountain road.

although some co-operatives have been set up, they have not managed to maintain their initial success for a variety of reasons, including the corruption which is endemic throughout Peru and death threats and actual killings by vested interest groups, some extreme right-wing, others on the left. Each has an axe to grind, be it political or material. Here, even ordinary commerce is fraught with some danger — and life can be very cheap indeed.

Add to all of this the fact that there is no social welfare system at all and the lot of the poor Peruvian becomes starkly apparent. It becomes a simple matter of work, scrounge, steal or starve. Apart from the relief agencies, which in some areas are themselves under threat from terrorists, there is nobody to whom the underprivileged can turn. In Trujillo, the women doing their washing at a communal outdoor 'laundry' may seem cheerful enough, as indeed they are. Esperanza may be seen sitting contentedly breast-feeding small Miguel, but in reality she is wondering if there will be enough to feed her family tomorrow, and her smile as she returns your greeting masks the desperate anxiety she is feeling.

For her and thousands like her, there is no tomorrow. It is enough if they can get through today. Night brings overwhelming tiredness and blessed oblivion for a few brief hours. At dawn, the same problems, and perhaps worse, have to be tackled all over again.

Above: Whether the car is capable of motion is debatable, but mobile four-wheeled wrecks are not unusual. The local bus is, by Peruvian standards, better than most.

Facing page: Transport for three — but not many can afford such luxury.

From the Burro to the Jet

PERUVIANS must be the most marvellous mechanics in the world. Surely nobody else could keep running the extraordinary collection of battered vehicles of every description which are to be seen on the roads everywhere throughout the country. They range from huge and ancient American limousines to tiny tricycles, either motorised or pedal-pushed, which serve as conveyances for both people and goods. Among the most popular of the smaller cars is the Volkswagen Beetle, but in Peru, the Beetle seems to be some sort of special insect, bred for local conditions and maintained in running order when it has little else but the engine, wheels and seats. Some are even used as taxis, which seem to be governed by no regulations whatsoever. In the majority, the speedometer does not work, which is probably a blessing, because Peruvians drive on the horn and brakes anyway, and it is doubtful if any odometer could record the sort of mileage which most of these venerable vehicles have to their credit.

In general, they tend to be short of the odd wing

or the odd window glass. Windscreen wipers are unknown because there is no need for them. Bumpers, where they exist, must surely be used for what the name implies, because they are all battered almost beyond recognition, and things like hub-caps and exterior mirrors simply do not exist, because they would not last very long. There is a brisk black market in spare parts and money to be made from those foolish enough to leave such things on display. If an essential part breaks in a Peruvian car, and if a replacement cannot be obtained through the ''normal'' channels, the owner and his friends will set to and make the part up from scrap metal, using all the skills of the metal worker and with precious little in the way of tools.

In one street in Trujillo, the sun blazes down on a veritable museum of old cars, all from the forties or fifties, and the majority of them American. A V-8 hearse suggested that perhaps this was part of the local undertaker's establishment. All have pieces missing, in the best Latin-American tradition. Yet the extraordinary thing is that all of them work almost daily for a living.

Public transport is little better. The majority of the buses are American Dodges, compact, sturdy and capable of coping with almost anything. Just as well, because some of those on the roads in Peru would be banned instantly here. The local bus from Trujillo

Young boys hitch a ride on the garbage truck, hoping for useful pickings at the dump.

to Huanchaco, for instance, is the most delapidated example of its kind that could possibly be found any-where, the bodywork so patched and rusted that it is all but unrecognisable. But every day it creaks and groans its way along the coast road on its mercifully short journey, loaded down with passengers who are no doubt glad that the whole of the trip is on the flat. On some buses, the tyres are so bald that the canvas is showing quite clearly; on others, bits of rubber fly off elderly tyres as the speed mounts to a bone-shaking 30 mph.

In the mountains, the mule or burro tends to be the transport king, carrying patiently, if not exactly cheer-fully, everything from crops to humans, from kindling to building materials. The burro is the poor man's beast of burden, just as in the cities and towns, the hand-cart or the tricycle serves the same purpose.

There are few trains in the country, the chief "express" being that running between Lima and Huancayo, while the tourist train to Machu Picchu, complete with oxygen masks to counter altitude sickness, can claim its own share of fame. All are now diesel-hauled, but curiously, the old steam engines were apparently far more efficient at high altitudes — something to do with air pressure at the combustion chamber . . . On a visit to Lima, a little group of us went to the railway terminal to see the trains, but the whole place was closed. Because it

The pedal tricycle is used for everything, from produce to people and, fortunately for Dad, most of Trujillo is flat.

is close to the Presidential Palace, armed guards were everywhere, and as we approached the station, one of them blew a whistle peremptorily and waved us away, all the while pointing a sub-machine gun at us. We didn't stop to ask why! Neither were we able to discover why there is no trunk line from Lima to Trujillo, which would seem to be an obvious route for such a venture. Only the bandit-infested Pan-American highway runs here, where goods lorries festoon themselves with spiky thorns to prevent pilferage of their loads en route.

Curiously enough, the air services in Peru can be very efficient indeed. The country is served by two airlines, Aeroperu and Faucett, the latter being a private company. Both use modern short-haul jets and service the area around Cuzco in the mornings and the north around Trujillo in the afternoons. The only problem is that conditions near Cuzco can be difficult for flying, so that planes which arrive there in the morning may be unable to fly out again immediately, and passengers at Trujillo could face a long wait. Here, as everywhere else in Peru, it is advisable to leave at least one day early if making a long journey, and especially if a connecting flight is to be picked up. There have been some air tragedies, but probably no more than in any other country, although flying over the jungle can be very hazardous. In this regard, some of the aged DC 3's

standing on the tarmac at Lima are scarcely calculated to create any sort of confidence, and they offer a shattering contrast to the sleek modern Jumbos which fly into Peru from other continents. Possibly they have very good mechanics too!

Facing page: People frequently travel in 'colectivos' or hackney cars, but in this instance an enterprising truck driver has packed in quite a crowd. Note the cheerful wave and general air of joviality.

Below: St. Christopher, patron saint of travellers, could find himself over-worked in Peruvian traffic!

Above: With spectacular sunsets such as this — at Huanchaco — is it any wonder that the antecedents of today's Peruvians were sun-worshippers!

Facing page: Worshippers at a shrine to Our Lady at Otusco. The mountain village is the scene of a huge annual religious 'fiesta'.

A Rich Loam of Belief

FROM time immemorial, man has worshipped some form of deity, some person, element or object, thought to be the supreme being, fount of all life and goodness, or occasionally, of evil and death, depending on the culture of the worshipper. This is as true of Peru as anywhere else. The Chimu tribe, for instance, builders of the huge complex of mud palaces at Chan Chan, outside Trujillo, may have used the twin symbols of fish and pelican as their emblems of plenty, but they worshipped the moon. To be more precise, and it is possibly a matter for some argument, they worshipped the reflection of the moon in a huge reservoir they used for irrigation.

More positively, the Incas were sun-worshippers, and this cult is still found in the currency of modern Peru. Almost worthless though it now is, it glories in the name *Inti*, the Inca name for 'sun', recalling the days when gold was precious only for ornamentation rather than for trade, when the Inca empire revered not the values of Mammon but the all-omnipotent influence of the centre of the solar system. There were, of

An old piety is evident in the faces of these communicants at the Ordination Mass of newly-ordained Fr. William Costa Serrano in Trujillo.

Very ornate candles are a feature of the many shrines in Peru.

course, dire rumours of the sacrifice of young maidens in order to forestall the wrath of the sun-god and to implore blessings and favours for the future. These are not uncommon in many cultures.

But formalised religion in the sense in which we know it today did not come to Peru until the advent of the Spanish Conquistadores. Pizarro may have been a brutish soldier of fortune, but he was accompanied by, or shortly followed by, groups of Spanish priests and monks who were no less zealous — except they were seeking souls rather than treasure. They tended, at times, to use the same methods as Pizarro.

While some historians would leave us vivid pictures of grim-faced Jesuits hounding the poor Peruvians with the Gospels in one hand and a sword in the other, the Inquisition certainly did reach Peru, being centred in Lima. The excesses of these early men of God were no less in Peru than in Europe, but it is only fair to say that the bulk of Peruvians embraced the faith willingly enough.

Nowhere is the evidence of the Spanish invasion now more apparent than in the sphere of religion. The Spaniards tended to build their Peruvian cities and towns just as they did at home; the focal point of every community is the *Plaza de Armas*, the great square around which are built the government offices, the chief hotel — and the church. To this very day, when

The traditional culture of the mountain people is transferred to the parish of El Buen Pastor on Procession Day. As these pictures show, the church is decorated, special costumes are worn and a carnival atmosphere prevails.

*Painted faces, chains and strange garb based on old traditions
are usual during the Procession.*

Streets become a riot of colour as the 'gipsy' procession advances,
usually to the haunting music of Peruvian instruments.

a new community springs up in the desert outside Trujillo, the first thing to be done is to locate the Plaza. This has been of some small benefit to our missionaries, because Peruvian insistence on following the old Spanish tradition often means that one of the best sites is reserved for the church.

So it is that even in remote, mountain communities, there are churches, or at least church buildings, some in decay or already ruined, either through disuse and neglect or by act of God such as earthquake or mudslide. The problem about the strength of the Spanish church was that it was essentially an alien institution, staffed in the main by Spanish clergy, without any deep roots in Peru itself. At the time of independence in 1820, many of the clergy fled, fearful perhaps of the consequences of instability and uncertainty.

The Church, as a body politic, became almost non-existent overnight. The beautiful Spanish-Colonial buildings began to rot, or to be used as storehouses and barns. Worst of all, many communities simply had no priests, and the few remaining, either Spanish or native Peruvian, simply could not hope to cater for the needs of their flock.

Some of the beautiful Spanish-colonial style churches in Trujillo and (bottom right) Otusco, where a new church has been built alongside an earlier one destroyed in an earthquake.

It took many years to restore what might be described as organised Catholicism as we know it and even then, the scarcity of priests is the greatest difficulty to be faced by the Peruvian church. Some 60% of priests in modern Peru come from overseas.

Today, in the Andean town of Otusco, there is only one church and one priest, a Franciscan from Madrid who is no longer young, who has to carry a huge pastoral burden and who is also fearful of the ever-present threat from the *Sendero Luminoso* guerillas. He is a man of immense courage in the face of great loneliness, but in the mountains, there are others like him. Other places still have no priests at all.

In spite of this, the majority of Peruvians will assert that they are good Catholics, even though they may not actually practise, largely through no fault of their own. It was not uncommon, in the Cork and Ross parishes in Trujillo, in recent times to find mass baptisms, with several hundred people of all ages receiving the Sacrament. Nowadays, not everybody goes to Mass every Sunday, even though they may have Sacred Heart pictures in their tiny homes and little statues of the Blessed Virgin in their battered cars. Those who do practise, however, are very dedicated indeed and very deeply involved. Mass in Trujillo lasts for at least an hour and the congregation will feel cheated if it is any shorter. They join in vociferously and the throbbing,

rhythmic sacred music is something that remains in the mind forever. There is great joy here, great celebration and a great sense of a living faith.

Just as life in Peru is very basic, so now is religion. The Church may have brought education and moves towards better living, but it also has to cope with the normal spiritual and temporal problems of communities where often there is no-one to turn to in time of trouble except the priest. People are born and have to be baptised; they die and have to be given a Christian burial. In between, they are beset with all of the woes of the human condition, greatly magnified by the circumstances in which they find themselves. So they tend to use every opportunity for rejoicing and a local saint's feast-day becomes an occasion for celebration which can last for days. But behind all the outward show of public homage, there is deep-rooted piety of the type that brought our own people safely through the evils of the Penal Laws. The faith will live on in Peru. Given enough priests, the Church Suffering of today will become the Church Triumphant of tomorrow. The rich, deep loam of belief is there. It needs only labourers to cultivate it.

In Peru, all is not equal even in death, as these pictures of cemeteries show. Left: the flowers and vaults of the better off, while (facing page) the poor lie in the desert sand.

DESERT MISSION

The grave of Ven. Archdeacon Tom Duggan near Lima has a special significance for the Cork and Ross Mission. Were it not for his death, Bishop Lucey may never have seen, at first-hand, the conditions which persuaded him to establish the Mission.

Facing page: Bishop Lucey with the late Archbishop Jurgens of Trujillo and Fr. Michael Murphy (now Bishop Murphy) in the early days.

SIXTY-EIGHT

Making the Desert Blossom

THE story of the foundation and development of the Cork and Ross mission in Peru is one of those epics which lay hidden for many years, partly because those involved were simply too busy with the task in hand to publicise either the mission or their own adventures, and also because over the years the whole project had become something of a *fait acompli*; it was there, it was working, it was being supported from home in terms of both manpower and finance and it was accepted as part of the order of things within the diocese. Yet, it was an extraordinary tale of high courage and endeavour, of trial and sometimes minor error, of infinite patience and above all, of faith and love. It is the story of a little band of men and women wrestling with strange and unforgiving conditions in a strange environment; of a courageous Bishop who saw a clear need to help the underprivileged both spiritually and materially and who decided that their call simply could not be ignored, no matter what the cost or the risk. It all began 25 years ago. It is still going on.

Digging the first sod for the Bon Secours Convent.

Left: Srs. Damian and Lawrence, two of the first Mercy Sisters to arrive from St. Maries of the Isle, Cork.

Facing page: Bishop Lucey waves goodbye as he leaves for home, following a visit to the Mission.

The mission could be said to have started with an historic meeting between the late Bishop of Cork and Ross, Most Rev. Dr. Cornelius Lucey and Cardinal Cushing of Boston in 1953, after which an enduring friendship was fostered between the two men. The Cardinal was at that time aware of the spiritual poverty of countries like Brazil and Peru and to combat this, he founded, in 1958, the Society of St. James the Apostle. Soon, volunteer priests were staffing missions in Bolivia, Ecuador and Peru. They were not alone, because a group of Irish Columban Fathers had been in Peru since 1952, but it was becoming clear that more and more priests would be needed. In 1961, Cardinal Cushing came to Cork and stayed with Dr. Lucey. Inevitably, there was talk of the missions, and Bishop Lucey began to wonder if some local priests might volunteer. He began, in typically cautious vein, to take some soundings.

It was to Father Michael Crowley, then stationed in Blackrock, that he turned first, apparently because Fr. Crowley had fluent Spanish! Quietly, he put the word about and in a series of weekly meetings with the Bishop, he was able to report that there was no shortage of volunteers. Within months, Fathers Crowley, Michael Murphy (now Bishop Murphy) and Patrick Leader were off to Peru to join the Society of St. James. At this point, it is impossible to ignore one of the most extraordinary events in the saga, because it had a

Bishop Murphy (facing page) laying hands on Father William Costa Serrano during his ordination and (above) concelebrating the Ordination Mass with Archbishop Manuel Prado of Trujillo and Fr. Costa.

distinct bearing on what was to follow, apart altogether from the fact that it is a compelling drama in its own right. The much-loved Archdeacon Tom Duggan, then aged 71, persuaded Bishop Lucey to allow him to go to Peru, in a gesture that was as heroic as it was unprecedented. The Bishop was both astounded and reluctant. The Archdeacon was elderly, he had no Spanish — he was scarcely a suitable candidate. But he was equally iron-willed and eventually Dr. Lucey, "reluctantly but admiringly" gave way. Archdeacon Tom headed off to Lima, where within weeks, on December 17th, 1961, he died. Significant events were to follow.

Dr. Lucey went to Lima to attend the funeral and while there he met Archbishop Silva of Trujillo, "an indefatigable fisher of men for Peru". He and some of the Cork priests, including Father Crowley, took the Bishop on a tour of the poor districts of Lima, an experience which left the Bishop shattered. He was later to write: "I little thought, when leaving Peru that December night, that I would ever see it again. But the events and contacts and impressions of the previous two days were conspiring that I should." Back at home, Peru simply refused to go away and Bishop Lucey continued to agonise about it. His feelings were in no way eased when Fathers Crowley and Murphy returned home in 1964 and reported to him. After lengthy discussion, it was decided that Cork and Ross could no longer stand aside from the enormous involvement and the even more enormous task of setting up its own mission in Peru. Dr. Lucey summed up his thoughts in the now well known remark: "You know you must get down to the job of channelling some of the plenty from here to those in want there, or your belief that we and they are the one people of God is just a matter of words and phrases only." He was honest enough to admit, however, that as Bishop, the decision had to be his "but as priests with experience of work in Peru and as men who would have to bear the heat and burden of the day, my decision would inevitably have to reflect theirs". It did. The groundswell of support was there, even though some of the problems were now known, having been experienced at first hand, and while Dr. Lucey immediately wrote to the Peruvian Nuncio, conveying his decision to initiate the Cork and Ross Diocesan Mission in Peru, the difficulties were only beginning.

At that stage, with the decision taken, there was a sort of heady innocence about the whole affair. The Nuncio wrote to say there was no shortage of places to go, listing more than a score, all in dire need of priests. "We scanned these, looking for a place in the lowlands with a population of about 30,000, all Spanish-speaking, not too isolated or remote", wrote Dr. Lucey. It seemed easy, but another conspiracy was at hand.

The work of the church never ceases.
Left: Bishop Murphy gives Communion to the handicapped
and (above) one of the Bon Secours Sisters is obviously much
loved by her young friends.

Fathers Crowley and Murphy, together with Fathers O'Sullivan and O'Donoghue, who joined them from the Society of St. James, began a scouting mission in Peru. They were joined by Bishop Lucey, and looked at various locations until they were met in Trujillo by the Vicar General, Mgr. Calderon, who in a "throwaway" comment, suggested that they might like to see some of the *barriadas* of El Porvenir and La Esperanza. Without knowing it, they were being "directed", if not actually blackmailed, emotionally! Seeing these areas, Dr. Lucey and his priests decided to look no further. These were surely the places most in need. Dr. Lucey noted: "It was a brave decision. Not for me. I would soon be safely and comfortably back home in Cork. But for them." On St. Patrick's Day 1965, the formal agreement setting up the Cork and Ross Mission in Trujillo was signed at the Nunciature in Lima. The new Society of *Padres Irlandeses de Santo Toribio* came into being. On April 3, 1965, Fathers Murphy and Crowley formally took charge of El Porvenir, with the latter soon moving into La Esperanza. The great work and the great adventure was under way at last.

Allied to the many priests from Cork and Ross who made their own contribution in the years that followed were five from the Diocese of Kerry and one from Cloyne, the late Fr. Paddy Hennessy.

The Church is seen as a light of hope to the people in the shanty-towns.

Facing page: Workers unload an invaluable cargo of milk powder from Ireland.

Most Rev. Dr. Michael Murphy, Bishop of Cork and Ross, with Sr. Teresa of the Mercy Order during his visit to Trujillo on the occasion of Fr. Costa's ordination in December 1988.

Facing page: Sisters of the Mercy Order, Irish and Peruvian, embrace Fr. Costa after his Ordination.

A Special Sort of Talent

WHILE it is quite true to say that the work of the mission in Peru could continue when staffed by priests only, it is equally apparent that without the presence of a group of determined and dedicated women, its effectiveness in many areas would be greatly diminished. There are so many things which women do so much better: dealing with the specific problems of their own gender, for instance; providing medical care, running primary schools and special institutions, organising, encouraging, goading, getting things done in a land where the word *mañana* and all that it symbolises needs a special sort of talent to overcome the lassitude. ''When I am inclined to throw up my hands in despair, Sister will somehow get those Peruvians moving'' recounts one priest in smiling recognition of the tenacity of spirit of the nuns.

So there they are, in the thick of it, but their story too is one of courage in the face of adversity, right from the very first day when, in April 1966, three Sisters of the Order of Mercy in Bantry, Srs. Aloysius, Gabriel and Columba arrived in Trujillo. Their long journey

Waiting for medical attention at a mission clinic.

Facing page: Some Peruvian teachers who have contributed enormously to the development of the Mission schools, photographed with Bishop Murphy, and (below) a group of teachers in a happy mood, as they enjoy a performance by some of their pupils.

on board the *SS Flamenco* was not without incident. The ship ran into a violent storm, and rudderless, managed to make the Peruvian coast. But the skipper refused to set into Salaverry, near Trujillo, and instead decided to head for Callao, the port of the capital, Lima. This meant that the good nuns and their tea-chests full of vital medicines had to be transported over the long haul of the Panamericana to Trujillo.

The nuns settled into a temporary house in Palermo, a middle-class suburb, while their convent was being built. Soon, the Bantry Sisters were joined by Mercy Sisters from Saint Maries of the Isle, and later by other Sisters from various Mercy Convents in Cork and Ross and Kerry. Meanwhile, on the credit side, the medical centre at El Buen Pastor was up and running.

Reinforcements were at hand. In September 1966, the Mother General of the Order of the Bon Secours, Mother Angelina, arrived in Peru with Sr. Rose Anne to set up a foundation there. These nuns do not hang about . . . two months later, four Sisters of the Order were busy at language school, Srs. de Sales, Joseph Finbarr, Felim and Columba. As the years went by, two Presentation Sisters worked for a time with the Bon Secours Mission. Twenty-four years later, Sr. Columba of the Bon Secours Order and Sr. Lawrence of the Mercy Order are still busy in the parishes of Trujillo, an extraordinary record of service and dedication.

A great deal has happened in the meantime. Both congregations have many Peruvian postulants and some nuns already professed. They are jolly young people, full of life and vigour, taking seriously things which must be taken seriously, but ever ready to laugh and sing. They will, at the drop of a coif, pick up a guitar and burst into 'Mi Peru' in the same way that a Corkonian will sing 'The Banks', except that these young ladies need far less persuasion. One is an accomplished Irish dancer . . . but that is another story!

Not only are they busy, these Irish and Peruvian Sisters, they are also very inventive. They have to be. "We have very few medicines, not enough to go around, so we make some of our own. We have used herbs to make up cures for coughs and burns and these, especially, have been successful. They also cost nothing."

They provide two vital services — medical care and education. It is impossible to over-estimate the value of each, in a land where otherwise they would be all but non-existent. Visit any of the twelve schools in the care of the mission and the difference between them and the State-run institutions is immediately apparent, the latter being run-down for want of funds while the former compare with anything here at home. This is due, in no small measure, to the magnificent work of over 100 local teachers who staff the mission schools, and whose dedication has, over the years, gone beyond the call of duty.

In Peru, to be ill is to face death. It is as stark as that. People needing an operation, for instance, will not even be allowed inside the door of the hospital until relatives have themselves bought all the necessary drugs and equipment — and that means everything, right down to rubber surgical gloves. ''What happens if they cannot afford it?'' ''Then they are left to die.''

That, of course, is the extreme, but at a slightly lesser level, the Sisters work in various medical centres and in a small maternity unit, where they battle against all sorts of ailments, especially tuberculosis, which is widespread. A small contribution is usually sought, but nobody is turned away and there are endless tales of emergency treatment. Maria had a baby last night, but the mother and child are seriously ill and they have no money. Word reaches the medical centre. ''Get the wagon and bring them down here immediately; we will have to see what we can do . . .'' In spite of shortages of almost everything, the mother and child survive; yet another battle is won, even though some may be lost.

There are sewing and typing classes, where the young Peruvians are proud of their prowess and rightly so, judging by the standard of work turned out. But above all, this sort of education gives them the hope of a better future, of real work, or real income, small though it may be by Western standards. At a place called Santo Toribio there is a small special school for the handicapped and everywhere, of course, the business of preparing children for the Sacraments goes on.

It all adds up to an unobtrusive sort of powerhouse of activity and achievement, of work, prayer and total dedication and above all, of love of ''the least of these''. The miracle is that amid so much deprivation which has to be coped with daily, amid all the hardships and shortages and frustrations caused by lack of facilities, these remarkable women are so cheerful — and their contribution so truly enormous.

Peruvian Bon Secours Sister Rocio cares for a baby at one of the medical centres.

A special class for handicapped children in progress at one of the schools.
Without such facilities, these young people would be totally neglected.

Fr. Michael Nyhan conducts a Baptism ceremony. Peruvians, through no fault of their own, are often mature when baptised.

Facing page: Priest of the future — Fr. Costa in contemplation during his Ordination.

Optimism and Faith

THE desert sands run through the hour-glass of time. The hot Peruvian sun rises and sets. The years pass. One of the pioneering spirits of the Cork and Ross Mission in Trujillo, viewed recently in an old picture, had a mop of jet-black hair and a youthful visage. Now he is back in Peru for another stint, this time white-haired and with his undoubted energy belieing his years. Twenty-five years have passed . . .

During that time, a great many priests and nuns have come and gone, having made their own contribution to the work of the mission. Inevitably, they look back with a little wonder at it all, with some affection, because Peru grabs you and won't let you go; often with a little anxiety — did we do enough, could we have done more? Above all, they tend to ask: did we expect too much, too soon?

They know, as do missionaries all over the world, that success is a relative and often intangible thing and that even in its most apparent form, it does not come quickly. It is easy to measure the concrete evidence of the growth and development of the mission: the churches, the schools, the small hospitals, the social

centres, the housing schemes.

It is not so easy to measure the success in terms of people brought to God, or the great outpouring of the Holy Spirit that has made it all possible, the simple faith, the act of vocation that sent men and women to spend themselves and part of their lives among the poor and underprivileged. But that success too is there. It is there in the packed churches, in the baptisms, marriages, First Communions and Confirmations, where once there were none.

It is there, above all, in the ordination last year of Father William Costa Serrano, of the gentle face and the anointed hands, the first young Peruvian to be ordained from the Cork and Ross Mission schools. In him, those who laboured to make the desert blossom find the consolation of knowing that they are perhaps witnessing the beginning of a process whereby the missionaries are working themselves out of a job.

Because that is the ultimate aim: to bring about a situation wherein the Church in Peru will be able to generate its own clergy once again, where there will be no further need for the men and women of Cork and Ross, and indeed, Kerry and Cloyne. That hope is there too in the number of Peruvian professed nuns and postulants in the convents in Trujillo — jolly young ladies, full of life and song and the gaiety of youth, and obviously very happy in their vocations.

*Mission schoolchildren elegantly demonstrate a traditional dance in
a picture that captures all the innocence and gaiety of youth.*

Above: Guinea pigs, a local delicacy, are now grown by a small co-operative set up by the mission.

Facing page: Ducks are also reared from chicks.

Politically and economically, there is precious little hope in Peru at the moment. Inflation is running at a staggering rate, where even thousands of percentages mean little any more. Basically, the country is unstable, in every way that instability is possible. The lot of the ordinary people disimproves with every passing day. All that is left to them is what optimism they can muster, and faith.

Too often, they must suffer violence: the violence of the *Sendero Luminoso*, of the armed forces and, above all, the violence of grinding poverty and deprivation. Their only hope lies in the relief agencies, but even their workers are now being threatened and killed by rebels who would rather see the 'peasants' starve, so that they might more easily be persuaded to join the 'revolution'.

Out of all this chaos, all that is left, indeed all that has been there for the past 25 years, is the mission and the men and women who staff it, bringing what material aid and skill they can, bringing, above all else, the eternal message of hope and love.

''By their works you shall know them'' and the impoverished people of Trujillo know of these works. They have only to look to the past, to the last 25 years, to find the inspiration and the hope for the future. The foundations built in that most unsuitable of areas, the sands of the desert, are good and strong. The work of building on them continues.

Members of the community co-op tend the larger ducks (facing page) while a co-op garden is tilled (above). These enterprises give the members a sense of purpose as well as a little profit.

Facing page: A local tailor and adobe brick-maker at work.

Above: ''Henceforth you shall be fishers of men . . .'' But at the moment, these Huanchaco fishermen are more concerned about mending their nets.

ICON Communications gratefully acknowledges the support of the following, whose generous sponsorship has made possible the publication of this book:

Aer Lingus.
Aer Rianta.
Apple Computer Ltd., Holyhill, Cork.
Ballinlough Credit Union, Cork.
Ballyphehane Credit Union, Cork.
Bank of Ireland.
Barn Restaurant, Lotamore, Cork.
Blarney Park Hotel, Blarney, Co. Cork.
Blarney Woollen Mills, Blarney, Co. Cork.
Bord Gáis Éireann.
Brian Wain & Associates, Architects, Douglas, Cork.
Cathedral Credit Union, Cork.
Cavanagh's (Fermoy) Ltd., Co. Cork.
Coakley's Atlantic Hotel, Garrettstown, Co. Cork.
Coca Cola Bottlers Ireland.
Cork Examiner Publications.
Cork Harbour Commissioners.
Patrick F. Coveney & Associates, Blackrock, Cork.
Crosshaven/Carrigaline Credit Union, Co. Cork.
De Leuw, Chadwick & Ó hEocha, Anglesea St., Cork.
Dúnlaoi Credit Union, Co. Cork.
Emerald Mail Order, Ballingeary, Co. Cork.
Mr. Gene Fitzgerald, M.E.P.
Gaeleo Ltd., Little Island, Cork.
Gurranabraher Credit Union, Cork.
Harrington Caterers Ltd., Cork.
Industrial Credit Corporation plc., Cork.
Irish International Trading Corporation Ltd., Cork.
Irish Steel Ltd., Haulbowline, Co. Cork.
P. W. Keane & Co. Ltd., Jewellers, Cork.
Kelly & Barry & Associates, Lower Glanmire Road, Cork.
Marina Oil Distributors Ltd., Bishopstown, Cork.
ICS Building Society, Patrick Street, Cork.

Brian Murphy O'Connor, Camden Place, Cork.
S. McD. Murphy & Partners, St. Patrick's Hill, Cork.
Muskerry Golf Club, Carrigrohane, Cork.
O'Brien & O'Flynn Ltd., Togher, Cork.
John O'Donovan & Associates, Model Farm Road, Cork.
J. W. O'Donovan & Co., South Mall, Cork.
O'Flynn Exhams & Partners, South Mall, Cork.
P. J. O'Hea & Co. Ltd., St. Patrick's Quay, Cork.
Kevin O'Leary (Bandon) Ltd., Bandon, Co. Cork.
Penn Chemicals B.V., Currabinny, Co. Cork.
E. G. Pettit & Co., Cork and Dublin.
Punch Holdings Ltd., Mayfield, Cork.
Ronan Daly Jermyn, South Mall, Cork.
Ronayne Shipping Ltd., Monahan Road, Cork.
Sea View House Hotel, Ballylickey, Co. Cork.
Sedgwick Dineen & Co, South Mall, Cork.
John Sisk & Son Ltd., Kinsale Road, Cork.
Stokes Kennedy Crowley, South Mall, Cork.
Smurfit Corrugated Ireland Ltd, Pouladuff Road, Cork.
Trócaire, Booterstown Ave., Blackrock, Co. Dublin.
Turners Cross Motors, Kinsale Road, Cork.
Upnor Ltd., Bishopstown, Cork.
West Cork Hotel, Skibbereen, Co. Cork.
P. Whelen & Co., Douglas Road, Cork.

Thanks to John A. Murray whose original ideal prompted this book.
Additional photography courtesy of Fr. Kevin O'Callaghan and Canon Mícheal ÓDálaigh. Film for Richard Mills' photography sponsored by Denis MacSweeney of Spectra/MacSweeney, Cork and Agfa Gevaert (Ireland) Ltd.

Liam O'Driscoll, **ICON Communications.**